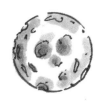

MEMOIRS OF
AN ANIMAL SHRINK

Russell Jones

S T A R

A STAR BOOK
Published by the Paperback Division of
W H ALLEN & Co Plc

FOR HANNAH

WITH THANKS TO SAM

A Star Book
Published in 1989
by the Paperback Division of
W.H. Allen & Co. Plc
Sekforde House, 175/9 St. John Street,
London, EC1V 4LL

Copyright © Russell Jones, 1989
Introduction and Epilogue copyright © Peter Neville, 1989

Printed in Great Britain

Design: Cecil Smith

ISBN 0 352 32586 0

CONTENTS

INTRODUCTION

BY PETER NEVILLE
Consultant in Animal Behaviour

Looking after a pet is good for you – from walking the dog to keep fit, to stroking the cat to relieve the stress of our modern hectic lifestyle. At the end of a long day what better welcome can there be than to have a dog or cat happy to see you home again?

The more we've come to depend on pets for our own sanity, the more we've come to observe them and wonder about their own state of mind. From the Animal Behaviourist's point of view, a new era has dawned where owners care enough about their pet's mental well-being to look for help if they begin behaving oddly. Complaints such as 'my dog has just wrecked my kitchen' or 'my cat is using my bed as a toilet' are good indications that an otherwise healthy, fun pet is having a spot of mental trouble which ought to be treated.

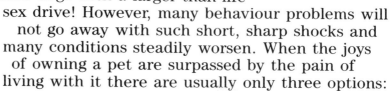

The vet can often help. One effective treatment they employ requires the use of a scalpel for those male dogs with a larger-than-life sex drive! However, many behaviour problems will not go away with such short, sharp shocks and many conditions steadily worsen. When the joys of owning a pet are surpassed by the pain of living with it there are usually only three options:

1) Give it to someone else (not charitable).
2) Ask a vet to dispatch it to that 'Great Kennel in the Sky' (not kind).
3) Try to modify the offending behaviour (not expensive).

Enter the Pet Psychologist (or Consultant in Animal Behaviour as he prefers to be known) on referral from the vet. A person with the knowledge and skill to look into all the influences on a pet's behaviour from genetics to the home environment, with special attention paid to the animal's relationship with the family. Understanding how the pack-evolved dog and the largely asocial cat have shaped their evolution to live in our den and with our social structure makes the prescribing of treatment to modify wayward behaviour that much easier.

But understanding why a problem occurs and how it can be cured is not enough. Motivating people to want to carry out the advice is the most important feature of being a pet 'shrink', especially with those owners who are at the end of their tether (or their dog's). Getting people to see the funny side of the problem can be a great help and if you can recount tales of even greater suffering experienced by other pet owners with similar problems (most now happily resolved), so much the better.

Everyone's pet from time to time indulges in very odd, sometimes very funny behaviour. My casebooks are crammed with vivid accounts of outrageous animal antics, and the most hilarious of these have been brought to life in this book by cartoonist and writer Russell Jones. During a chance meeting with him in a London restaurant where I had been treating the owner's dog, he showed a keen interest in my profession and I agreed to show him my casebooks. The following week he ransacked my office and having absorbed the contents of the filing cabinets, Russell demanded that the public should be told the truth about those animals whom he considers to be 'one brick short of a load', and so this book was born.

Except to say that each story is based on a *true* case that I've seen and treated over the years, what follows in this book is a total figment of Russell's imagination, and his speculations as to the cause of some of the conditions deserve an endorsement on his poet's licence. In a vain effort to preserve professional credibility, I have given the diagnosis of each case as it appears on my files, and have changed the names of my clients (so shamefully lampooned) to protect the innocent. Other than this, I wash my hands completely of what follows.

No doubt on publication day with my career in tatters, my professional image in sharp decline and with the bailiffs hammering on my door, I'll end up stretched out on my psychiatrist's couch as he desperately searches for ways to treat my depression – he could try reading me a couple of stories from this book!

Peter Neville BSc (Hons)
Consultant in Animal Behaviour
Surrey 3 June 1989

CATEGORIES

THE NERVOUS WRECKS

This section is devoted to that unfortunate group of pets whose nerves have been shattered by a hair-raising (or feather-raising) experience. From an eagle so terrified of heights she can't stop trembling to a huge ex-guard dog so fearful of anything larger than a horsefly he can't stop breaking wind, the stories in this chapter are truly heart-rending.

THE HEADBANGERS

A large, simple-minded group of animals who seem to find great pleasure indulging in mind boggling stupidity. It includes such classic exponents of this art as Colonel the Dobermann Pinscher, founder member of the 'Dumb Dog Club' and Tommy the Budgerigar who, anxious to avoid a dead-end job embarked on a career as a kamikaze pilot!

THE ATHLETES

As the title suggests this section concerns itself with those pets who display an athleticism above and beyond the call of duty. It includes marathon runners, mountaineers, tunnellers and a car chaser so skilled in the art that she's inspired poets and secured herself a place in the 'Vehicle Pursuers' Hall of Fame'.

THE SEXUALLY DEVIANT

Here we enter the twilight world of that seedy band of pets who heap shame upon the animal kingdom and bring crushing embarrassment to their owners. From those who've mounted frenzied assaults upon the clergy to those who've had their evil way with defenceless teddy bears, the list of indecent acts is as long and as grubby as a flasher's raincoat.

WARNING: Parental guidance is suggested for readers under sixteen as some stories contain explicit descriptions of extreme perversity.

THE 'OUT TO LUNCH' MOB

Condoms, cable-knit sweaters, mahogany commodes, wall tapestries and Afghan rugs are all in a day's eating for some pets! This section also includes one of the most bizarre cases on record: a dog who actually ate and seemed to enjoy a British Rail cheese sandwich!

THE CHRONICALLY INCONTINENT

A messy business this, requiring the reader to have a strong stomach. This chapter deals with the horrifying consequences resulting when chronic incontinence is combined with chronic incompetence!

THE TOTALLY DERANGED

The dictionary definition of 'totally' reads as follows, 'Completely, entirely and wholely'. The same dictionary defines 'deranged' as 'disturbed, muddled, unhinged and demented'.

Between pages 45 and 51 you'll find some classic examples of completely, entirely and wholely disturbed, insane, confused, muddled, unhinged and extremely demented animals.

THE HEAVY GANG

Most of the animals written about here would make the average American Pit Bull Terrier seem like a product of charm school. Within this section we find psychopaths, homicidal maniacs and feline contract killers standing cheek by jowl with an assortment of furry weirdos all suffering from severe personality defects.

As these stories pull no punches, this chapter is not recommended to the squeamish.

THE NERVOUS WRECKS

We open our casebook of nervous wrecks to find Lulu, an eagle from the Philippines. Earning her living display-flying at public functions, she ended up more nervous and wrecked than most following a terrifying close encounter at 400 feet. One afternoon as Lulu was preparing to execute her party piece, a fearless dive from great height onto her handler's wrist, a Royal Air Force Tornado bomber on a low-flying exercise thundered by not six feet from her starboard wing.

According to eye-witnesses, the glazed expression on the poor creature's face as she was led away from the bush into which she'd plummeted, was unforgettable.

Resisting all attempts by her handler to relaunch her career, Lulu now prefers walking to flying. Startled by noises above a whisper and terrified of heights, she sits trembling on a perch just two inches above the floor of a darkened cage, perhaps still pondering the nature of the anti-social beast that breathes smoke and flame, sounds like a thunderclap and flies at 300 miles an hour!

LULU

PHILIPPINE EAGLE –
FEMALE

Sound Phobic

BRUNO

GERMAN SHEPHERD
DOG – MALE

*Fear-induced
Expression of Wind*

A large fire-breathing ex-guard dog of German origin, Bruno could trace his family tree back to Himmler's S.S. However, one morning he suffered a complete breakdown when his bluff was called by a streetwise Maltese Terrier. According to his owner, the worst symptom of Bruno's condition was the uncontrollabe fits of wind-breaking which meant that the trembling hound was enveloped round the clock in the most appalling stench. On the strength of this talent, he entered the dog for the 1989 Eurovision Pong Contest where he managed second place behind the Yugoslavian entry, a foul-smelling Rottweiler from Belgrade.

BAMBER

CROSS-BRED CAT – MALE

*Victimisation By Other Cats
Due To Changed Profile*

Having been surgically separated from his tail following an accident with a milk float, Bamber looked forward to returning home to bore his friends to distraction with endless talk about his operation. Sadly, it was not to be. His clean-cut appearance became a great source of amusement to the other cats in the alley and, as a direct result of the ridicule they heaped upon him, Bamber developed a severe inferiority complex.

When last heard from, he was considering settling on the Isle of Man where at least he would be amongst his own kind.

After moving to a new home, Custer was careful to observe all the usual precautions before making his first excursion into the garden. Keen to do a spot of crop spraying and lay claim to the land that now belonged to him, his first task was to make a textbook exit through the cat flap. He decided to play it strictly by the rules, just like mother had taught him.

1. A five minute stare through the perspex to make sure that all was quiet outside. 2. Place head and one paw slowly through the flap. 3. A double burst of rapid sniffing to check for hidden perils. 4. Look right, look left, look right again. 5. If all seems clear, make a dash for the nearest cover.

Having followed these rules to the letter, the cat was about to complete section 5 by diving into a privet hedge when he was set upon by a foul posse of airborne bandits who made it their business to impress on the newcomer that this was to be Custer's Last Stand.

His physical injuries healed quickly but the mental scars resulting from the surprise attack remain. Section 4 of the 'Moggies Cat Flap Exiting Code' now reads, 'Look right, look left, look up!'.

CUSTER

CROSS-BRED CAT – MALE

Housebound Due to Victimisation

ROGER

CROSS-BRED DOG

Lamp post Phobic

On catching sight of Roger, who could only be described as a shambling eyesore, few people would have disagreed with the claim that he displayed all the most hideous features of the one hundred and ten different breeds that made up his family tree.

A typical city mongrel, Roger was not only short on looks, he was also short on luck and what little of the latter the dog possessed ran out one evening as he was sniffing his way along an alley on a dustbin mugging exercise. Pausing to cock a leg against a favourite lamp post, Roger experienced a deep sense of shock as the power supply for the entire borough of Hackney in east London passed briefly through his hind quarters!

Staggering painfully home after this cruel experience, hair standing on end and his bark three octaves higher than normal, he was complimented by other dogs in the neighbourhood on how much his appearance had been improved by the new toilet-brush hairdo.

Shattered by his shocking experience, Roger, now a broken dog, restricts his leg-cocking to supermarket doorways and telephone kiosks.

THE HEADBANGERS

COLONEL

DOBERMANN – MALE

*Directional Incompetence
During Activity*

What finer, more constructive pastime could there be for a dog than to spend an afternoon in the park headbutting oak trees! Colonel the Dobermann considered it an art form.

Being a purist, he chose only those opponents with a girth in excess of seven feet and weighing more than five tons. When a suitable

"'ELLO SAILOR..!"

HUMPHREY

KING CHARLES CAVELIER
SPANIEL – MALE

Misdirected Hypersexuality

A founder member of the 'Fair Do's for Gay Mutts Movement', Humphrey the Cavelier Spaniel did much to promote the gay canine cause by 'coming out' so early in his young life. However, many mistakes were made in the early days, one of the more costly of which being the propositioning of a butch-looking Staghound one evening who, as fate would have it, not only possessed a vile temper but, sadly for Humphrey, also possessed an insatiable appetite for violence.

The injuries resulting from this encounter are remembered by his vet as being 'quite extensive'.

tree had been found and challenged, battle would commence, usually ending in exhaustion and stalemate. However, if the Colonel had picked on a particularly aggressive tree, he'd quite regularly be pounded into submission and had been seen on more than one occasion to pass blissfully into that state that unsuccessful boxers have come to know as *The Twilight Zone*.

Known to his fans as 'Ol' Brown Eyes', Tonto the German Shepherd decided when just a pup that there really was no business like show business. His stage was the family car and his repertoire contained something for everyone – from Gilbert and Sullivan to Jason and Kylie.

His owner was forced to seek help following a journey from London to Basingstoke during which Tonto performed the entire score from *West Side Story*, complete with basic choreography! Rumour has it that his rendition of 'Maria' was so moving, the driver was forced onto the hard shoulder as the entire family was overcome with emotion.

..... AND DID IT MY WAY ! ....

TONTO
GERMAN SHEPHERD DOG –
MALE

In-Car Vocalisation

GEMINI

HORSE

*Irritability Due to
Deprivation of Routine*

When just a young foal, Gemini decided to run away from home to 'take the King's shilling' and immerse himself in the rough and tumble of army life. Misleading the selection board about his age by refusing to let the veterinary surgeon count his teeth, he was accepted into the ranks and he gave up his life as a civilian nag in exchange for two square meals a day and a rub-down every morning administered by a spotty Lance Corporal. Gemini was trained to march up and down behind a military band, dropping the occasional rose-growers' present along the way, and this he did with pride and precision for many years.

However, all good things come to an end and after a long and illustrious career, he was put out to grass in a retirement home in the country.

Things did not go well. Becoming testy and bad tempered, he disrupted the routine of the stables, turning his nose up at the food and refusing to be mucked out. Help was eventually sought and following a long investigation it was decided that Gemini was probably missing the military music to which he'd become so accustomed. So, a sound system was swiftly wired up in his stall and before long a selection of Sousa marches was ringing out around the stable yard.

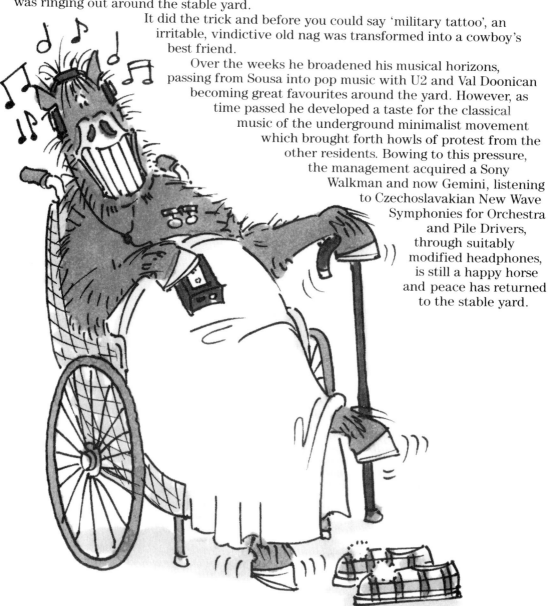

It did the trick and before you could say 'military tattoo', an irritable, vindictive old nag was transformed into a cowboy's best friend.

Over the weeks he broadened his musical horizons, passing from Sousa into pop music with U2 and Val Doonican becoming great favourites around the yard. However, as time passed he developed a taste for the classical music of the underground minimalist movement which brought forth howls of protest from the other residents. Bowing to this pressure, the management acquired a Sony Walkman and now Gemini, listening to Czechoslavakian New Wave Symphonies for Orchestra and Pile Drivers, through suitably modified headphones, is still a happy horse and peace has returned to the stable yard.

JAKE

GREEN PARROT

Alcohol Addiction

Brought up in a seafront pub where his cage hung from a ceiling beam, Jake the parrot, having observed from on high the mind-boggling spectacle of a Saturday night in the public bar, vowed that strong drink would never pass his beak.

However, he was forced from the straight and narrow one evening when a customer, full of goodwill and a gallon of rough cider, laced the bird's water trough with a double measure of Green Chartreuse.

It was the thin end of the wedge. Ten minutes later, Jake burst into an emotional but tuneless rendition of 'Danny Boy' forcing the customers to shower his cage with bread rolls and beer mats in an effort to silence him and from that day forth, Jake went steadily down hill. Drinking anything from cocktails to cleaning fluid he could often be seen storming around his cage in a drunken frenzy, smashing mirrors and perches and spraying customers with abuse and seed husks.

The landlord sought help when Jake, sobbing uncontrollably began launching into late night, maudlin monologues about his sad decline, sending the customers rushing for the exits in search of a pub without a parrot.

WILF

CROSS-BRED DOG

Idiopathic Obsession

Some dogs become professional models chasing rosettes and silverware, others professional athletes chasing paper-boys and postmen, but Wilf, looking for a life in the fast lane packed with glamour and excitement, became a building inspector.

Regarded by his owner as a reincarnated bricklayer, the dog was unable to pass a wall without first inspecting it in minute detail. Work that was up to scratch was given a bark of approval, but shoddy, slap-happy bricklaying, below the standard laid down in section two, paragraph four of the building regulations was greeted with a fierce howling and tutting.

Becoming dismayed by what Wilf considered to be the growing menace of sloppy workmanship, he became an on-site inspector, making it his business to oversee work on a garden wall being built for neighbours. Growling menacingly if each course was not perfectly laid, the bricklayer and his hod-carrier became so terrified of making an error that the wall took six months to complete instead of the scheduled three days. However, although progress was painfully slow, the finished product was built to such a degree of accuracy that the owner bestowed it on the nation and it's now on permanent display in The Science Museum.

MABEL

PARROT – PRESUMED
FEMALE

Self-Mutilation

We've all trimmed our hair from time to time even though we're aware that the results can well be tragic. In the space of five snips and ten seconds we've reduced ourselves from something resembling a normal human being to something resembling a special effect from *Nightmare on Elm Street*. So it was with Mabel, a green parrot from Portsmouth who insisted on trimming herself at least twice weekly. Mabel's style was known as the 'Buxted Oven-Ready Look' and was quite popular for a time with the more trendy sections of the parrot world.

If there's one thing worse than giving yourself a bad haircut it's having a hairdresser do it for you! The day Rupert the Rastafarian, a long-haired Burmese, wandered into a pool of soft tar was the day his life took a dramatic turn for the worse. With black goo clinging to his dreadlocks, he was whisked to the local surgery where the junior partner administered a National Health hatchet job so appalling, that when Rupert emerged through his cat-flap an hour later, there was panic in the streets. The unfortunate moggie took months to come to terms with his hideous hairdo but as his dreadlocks returned so happily did Rupert's self-confidence.

RUPERT

PERSIAN CAT – MALE

Trauma-Induced Incompetence

TOMMY

BUDGERIGAR – MALE

In-Flight Misjudgement

After a hard morning's squawking and millet crunching, Tommy the budgerigar liked nothing better than to relax in a bowl of warm porridge. Inspired by the Japanese kamikaze pilots of World War II, he'd climb to ceiling height and circle slowly above the breakfast table before plummeting fearlessly into somebody's Quaker Oats. Badly misjudging his dive one morning, Tommy splashed down into a mug of extremely hot tea. According to those gathered for breakfast, his rocket-like exit from the receptacle was so spectacular that it brought forth a spontaneous and well-deserved round of applause.

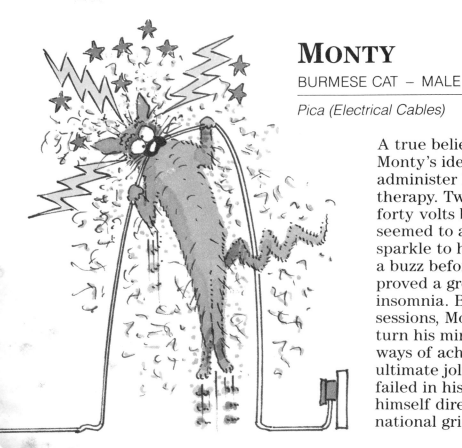

MONTY

BURMESE CAT – MALE

Pica (Electrical Cables)

A true believer in self-help, Monty's idea of fun was to administer his own shock therapy. Two hundred and forty volts before lunch seemed to add a certain sparkle to his afternoon and a buzz before bedtime proved a great help with his insomnia. Between therapy sessions, Monty would often turn his mind to devising ways of achieving the ultimate jolt, but has so far failed in his attempts to plug himself directly into the national grid.

BONZO

GREAT DANE DOG

Physical Lack of Control

Why would a branch of the Young Farmers Club bestow a 1st prize rosette on a small pregnant woman and a Great Dane? Read on.

Realising his owner, Mrs X, was heavy with child, Bonzo, a sensitive and caring Great Dane whose four and a half ton body was controlled by a one and a half ounce brain, decided to make it his business to help out in any way he could. One of his 'brighter' ideas was to employ a technique known as 'surfboarding' in order to take the weight off his owner's feet. On a trip to the supermarket for instance, this involved gathering momentum along the pavement until Mrs X lost her footing and was converted quickly and effortlessly into a human surfboard. His owner's squeals of delight and pleadings for him not to stop drove Bonzo on to attain astonishing speeds as they rode the big one to the shops.

One day, feeling particularly helpful, Bonzo decided to take the scenic route, and after surfboarding Mrs X through her third hedgerow they unwittingly joined a ploughing competition organised by the Young Farmers Club. Egged on by the assembled gaggle of tweed-suited young fogeys, Bonzo and Mrs X ploughed a fifteen acre field in five minutes flat and the judges, awarding points for speed and straightness of furrow, had no

WILLY

CROSS-BRED DOG

Separation Anxiety

The day Mr X decided to buy a new delivery van was the day his dog decided to embark on a new career. In the time it took his owner to eat a three course meal, Willy the cross-bred turned into Sergio Macaroni, Italian body stylist extraordinaire.

The first morning out in the new van with his faithful companion, Mr X returned from lunch to find that Willy had completely remodelled the cab producing what can only be described as a totally new and exciting design concept. The roof had been streamlined and lowered four inches, air conditioning had been provided by the removal of the windscreen and most eye-catching of all, the interior had been given a wonderfully *avant-garde* restyle known as the 'ripped and tattered look'.

Overcome, Mr X, hands outstretched, knuckles white, rushed towards his dog in an effort to thank him for a job well done but Willy, being a modest sort of hound, took off through the shattered windscreen refusing to accept the congratulations that were about to be heaped upon him.

Now Mr X, well wrapped-up against the numbing efficiency of his new air conditioning system, can often be seen searching the highways and by-ways for the missing dog, and it is rumoured that he's acquired a shotgun to present to Willy as a small token of his appreciation.

hesitation in awarding the duo
first prize.

Readers will be relieved to hear that
Mrs X gave birth to a very healthy child
who spends most of his time happily
surboarding with Bonzo down to
the ice-cream parlour.

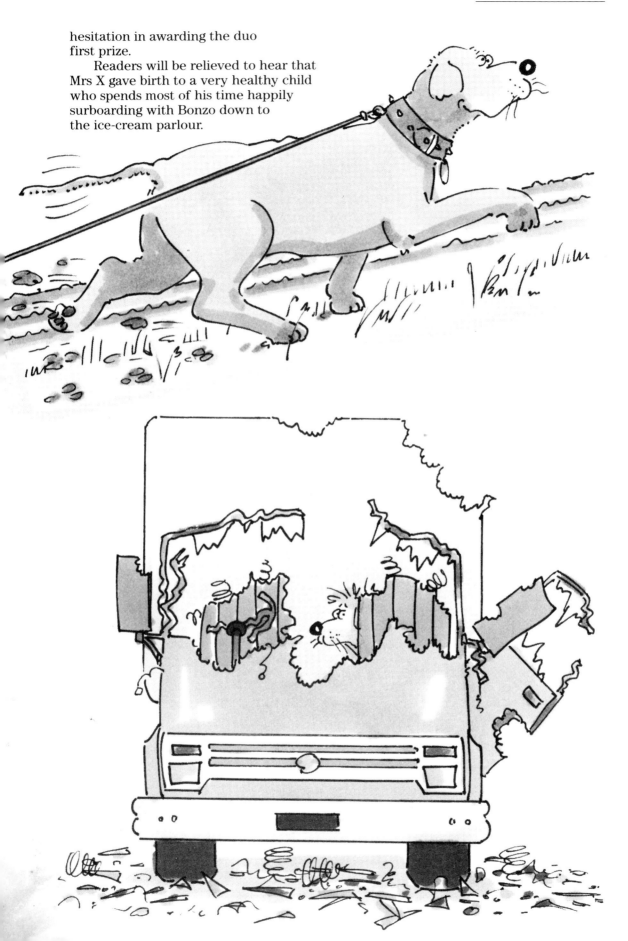

BULLET

CROSS-BRED CAT – MALE

Excessive Predatory Behaviour

GERALD

JACK RUSSELL – MALE

Dominance (Preventing Owner From Leaving House)

Gerald didn't like his owner going out at night without him. Not understanding that a dinner-dance at the local rotary club was no place for a Jack Russell, he decided one evening to deny the party-goer access to his dinner jacket until his demands for a night out on the tiles were met. As time passed, Gerald's behaviour became more aggressive and his unhappy owner was forced to seek help when one evening, fearing for his life if he approached his tuxedo, he was forced to turn up and deliver a speech at the firm's annual do in a Union Jack teeshirt and a pair of jogging pants.

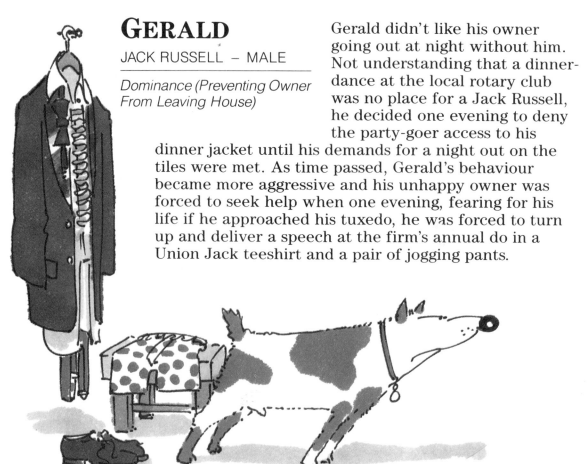

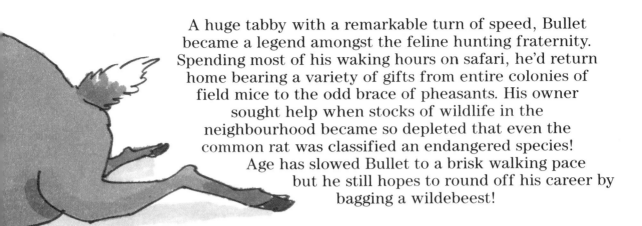

A huge tabby with a remarkable turn of speed, Bullet became a legend amongst the feline hunting fraternity. Spending most of his waking hours on safari, he'd return home bearing a variety of gifts from entire colonies of field mice to the odd brace of pheasants. His owner sought help when stocks of wildlife in the neighbourhood became so depleted that even the common rat was classified an endangered species! Age has slowed Bullet to a brisk walking pace but he still hopes to round off his career by bagging a wildebeest!

Just as some people fall in love with their Porsche or their loft conversion, Dylan fell in love with rubbish. He'd defend the household dustbin resolutely against any threat, being particularly aggressive to the unfortunate people whose job it was to empty it every Tuesday and Friday.

Things came to a head when his owner was threatened with prosecution for harbouring household waste and Dylan himself accused of savaging council employees and stealing from rubbish trucks.

The latest news is that the dog remains on guard and the situation has deteriorated into a smelly stalemate.

DYLAN

MONGREL DOG – MALE

Food Guarding (Non-Specific)

RUFUS

CROSS-BRED DOG

Over-enthusiastic Pack Protection

Taken in by two elderly sisters as protection from thieves and robbers, Rufus took to life as a personal bodyguard with great enthusiasm.

Seeing himself as the last line of defence between his charges and the evil world outside, he graded the varying degrees of threat to the sisters on a scale of one to ten. Bottom of the list and to his mind posing the least threat, were those charming, happy-go-lucky members of the criminal fraternity who specialised in mugging old ladies, whilst top of the list, scoring a threat factor of ten was that sinister, depraved, malevolent bundle of human wickedness – the district nurse!

The sight of this smiling demon on the doorstep in her vile raincoat and evil little cap with silver badge twinkling menacingly like a third eye, would sound the red alert and drive the dog into a frenzy of activity. Herding the sisters into the safety of the back parlour, he'd fearlessly confront the monstrous apparition and summoning all his courage, chase it back down the garden path to where the noddy car was parked.

If one thing gave Rufus more pleasure than to see the cowardly toad struggling frantically with the driver's door, it was to watch her trying forty-nine different keys in the ignition out of her bunch of fifty as he sat on the bonnet, staring through the windscreen, rolling his eyes and giving a vivid impression of a hound in the final stages of hydrophobia.

Finally, with the help of key number fifty, the car would start, and accelerating from nought to one hundred and twenty-eight miles an hour in eight seconds flat, the district nurse would begin her journey back to the local health centre, and Rufus, wallowing in the satisfaction of another triumph of good over evil, would return to the house and rescue his beloved old ladies from the back parlour.

CLARENCE

CROSS-BRED DOG

*Dominance Aggression
(Pack Control)*

Just as some people find it therapeutic to study the splendours of The Great Barrier Reef by keeping a small goldfish trapped in a very small bowl, so Clarence found it therapeutic to observe the rich tapestry of human life by keeping a small family of people trapped in a very small family car. To his mind there was no better way to relax on a hot summer's afternoon than to gaze through the windows of a five door hatchback as the occupants, unable to escape and gasping for air, swam back and forth between the nodding dog on the rear parcel shelf and the furry dice decorating the rear view mirror.

One afternoon, having decided to move on to more ambitious projects, Clarence managed to trap fifty one people on board a London bus, thereby creating the first giant, two-tier human aquarium.

It took three hours of skilful negotiation on the part of the driver before the dog would agree to free the women and children, but it was early evening before he could be persuaded to release the rest of the passengers and allow them to swim home.

STANLEY

JACK RUSSELL DOG

*Aggressive Protection of
Acquired Privilege*

The first time Mr X attempted to join his new wife in bed to fulfil his matrimonial duties, he was confronted by her dog, a beady-eyed, bad-tempered Jack Russell by the name of Stanley, who made it perfectly clear to him that there was only room for one male in his owner's life. Mr X took the hint and spent the next three nights in an armchair, but on the fourth night, fed up and driven on by lust he attempted physically to sweep the dog aside. It proved to be a terrible blunder as the irritable mutt displayed all the fearless characteristics of his breed.

Quickly tattooing a set of teeth marks on the poor man's rump, Stanley took off in pursuit as Mr X, now driven on by fear, made for the stairs. Taking them six at a time, he managed to reach the back garden where he locked himself in the shed.

Stretched out uncomfortably across three bags of potting compost, he spent a miserable night in sub-zero temperatures. When rescued the following morning he was found to be suffering from frost bite, exposure and what can only be described as a delirious condition for when he was discovered he was in deep conversation with a rotary lawn mower.

Readers will be relieved to hear that the frost bite did not extend to vital organs and that Mr X is now the proud father of a baby boy.

THE ATHLETES

NELLY

BORDER COLLIE – FEMALE

Car Chasing (Predatory)

An incurable car chaser from Ireland, Nelly was considered by her peers to be the complete professional, the car chasers' car chaser! Coming to grief one day due to a rare lapse in concentration, a local poet penned the following lines in admiration.

A Collie from Kerry called Nelly
Would rather chase cars than watch telly
Like a stampeding horse
She'd take after a Porsche
And pursue it with maximum welly!

One day with an ear-splitting roar
An exotic two-seater full bore
Lost control on a bend
Catching Nelly's front end
Now she chases on three legs not four!

JEZEBEL

PEKINESE – FEMALE

Jogger Chaser

Whilst Nelly was an incurable car chaser, Jezebel a bad tempered anti-social Pekinese was an incurable jogger chaser. Regarding all runners as disturbers of the peace in a public park she'd long considered her own, Jezebel chased them with the single-minded aggression of a dog possessed. Fuelled by sheer terror whilst being pursued by the beast, it's said that one gaggle of elderly joggers from a nearby retirement home reached and sustained speeds in excess of 30 miles per hour one afternoon, making a mockery of Ben Johnson's claim to being the fastest human being ever!

CASEY

BORDER COLLIE –
FEMALE

Misplaced Herding Instinct

A dog driven by the hunter's instinct, Casey loved the wide open spaces. Her Serengeti was the local school playground and her prey the small inhabitants of this wild and dangerous concrete jungle. She looked forward most of all to the rainy season when huge herds of tiny uniformed beasts would migrate south towards the playing fields where mother nature would display her cruel

beauty in a deadly game of cat and mouse.

One memorable day she completed a fabulous sequence of moves that would have scored a perfect ten in any dog trial. Rounding up the entire junior netball team, she herded them into the shedding ring and in one skilful operation separated the 'Hard-working and conscientious with a natural flair for Maths, English, Chemistry, Physics, Sports, Music and Art. A joy to teach, a credit to the uniform' from the 'To be frank, a no-hoper. Totally disruptive in class and a bad influence on fellow pupils, he refuses point blank to take even a passing interest in school activities. Seemingly unable to grasp the basics of the Queen's English he could, however, undoubtedly compile a reference book of its obscenities' into two neat groups and kept them separated until the lunch bell sounded a truce.

Professional help was called in following the school's sports day when thirty cross-country runners failed to return to base. A search party found them later that evening penned in the bicycle shed waiting patiently to be herded single-file towards the sheep dip.

POLLY AND JOCK

BORDER COLLIES, MALE AND FEMALE

Excessive Uncontrolled Herding Behaviour

Polly and Jock found their excitement difficult to contain on spying the first of the woolly bobble hats, the vomit-yellow cagoules and the dun-coloured cable-knits that heralded the start of the rambling season.

Experts at heading off at the pass, stalking, rounding up and penning, the dynamic duo, working as a team, made life thoroughly miserable for everyone walking in the surrounding hill country. All were considered fair game from gaggles of weekend wanderers (easily recognised by their Perrier water and personal stereos), to bands of serious walkers (easily recognised by their olive green boots – the type that have more lace holes than a dog's got fleas).

Walkers who couldn't stand the fierce pace demanded by the main group would often fall behind with nothing between them and Valhalla but a canteen of water and a packet of cream crackers. Here the dogs were in their element. The wretched band of stragglers would be mercilessly rounded up and herded for miles until exhausted and fed up they'd find themselves cornered with seemingly no hope of escape.

There was however one situation guaranteed to force Polly and Jock to break off the action. This occurred when the gang of prisoners, beginning to lose heart and despairing of ever being rescued, would be rallied by the strongest member with his trusty guitar. On hearing a trembling, high-pitched female voice break into 'How many roads must a man walk down . . .', the dogs, howling for mercy would run home in panic, arriving just in time for tea.

Most cats are content to contain their curiosity within a fifty metre radius of the food bowl. Not so Buster the happy wanderer. Departing twice weekly along the railway embankment at the foot of his garden, this large, rugged ginger tom, driven relentlessly onward by the explorer's urge to ford rivers, traverse valleys and climb mountains, would wander up to ten miles from home.

Using the old 'I'm just a poor lost pussy cat' routine on elderly ladies along his route, Buster would return home surprisingly well fed and healthy. Next year, following a full-scale expedition along the

BUSTER

CROSS-BRED CAT – MALE – UNNEUTERED

Abnormal Roaming – Territorial

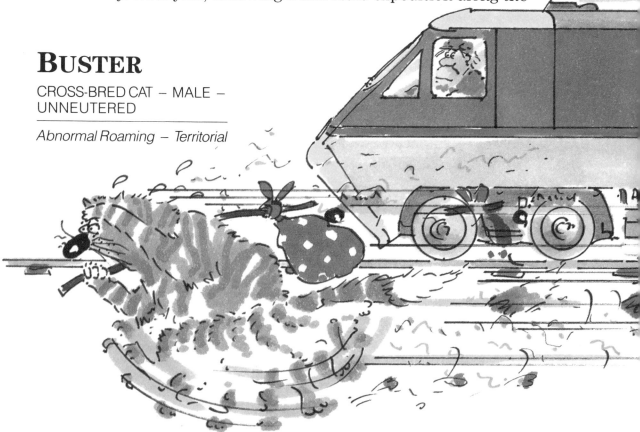

DANDY

COLLIE CROSS-BREED – FEMALE

Severe Tail Chasing With Self-Mutilation

Some dogs devote their lives to rescuing people from snowdrifts, others to guiding blind people from A to B. Dandy decided at an early age to devote her's to chasing her tail.

Pausing only for light refreshment, nothing else was allowed to interrupt the pursuit. A mathematician friend of the family once calculated that in order for Dandy to catch up with the tail and establish once and for all to whom it belonged, she would have to attain a speed of 127 revolutions per minute. Realising the impossibility of this task the dog hatched a cunning plot. Suddenly stopping one day she quickly reversed her direction thereby catching the tail completely by surprise!

embankment to seek out primitive cultures rumoured to exist beyond Luton and Dunstable, Buster plans to broaden his horizons with a back-packing trip to the Hindu Kush with Sir Laurens Van der Post.

Dandy seized her opportunity and during a brief struggle inflicted heavy damage on the appendage.

When the stitches had been removed she returned to the chase, but found that the tail, having learned from its mistake had become much more difficult to outwit!

CHALKY

CROSS-BRED DOG – MALE

*Androgen-Induced Roaming
Acquired Privilege*

Known as the Great Escaper, Chalky overcame all attempts by his family to confine him to the house and garden. A hedonist totally devoted to the pursuit of the sex, drugs and rock 'n' roll life that lay on the other side of the garden fence, nothing could be done to imprison him for long and stem the flood of complaints concerning the dog's bad behaviour around the neighbourhood.

A master of camouflage and tunnelling, he could scramble over a ten foot fence and blend chameleon-like into the background on the other side.

His reputation as the next Steve McQueen was firmly established when his owner's house dramatically subsided one morning, leading to the discovery of an intricate network of tunnels below. Seven led directly to the kennels of the most attractive females in the area, two into the cellars of the local pubs, one went right into the heart of Soho, and the most ambitious project led into the Paris red-light district.

Employed now as an advisor on the Channel Tunnel, Chalky spends his spare time jumping barbed wire fences on stolen motorbikes in a further attempt to emulate his hero.

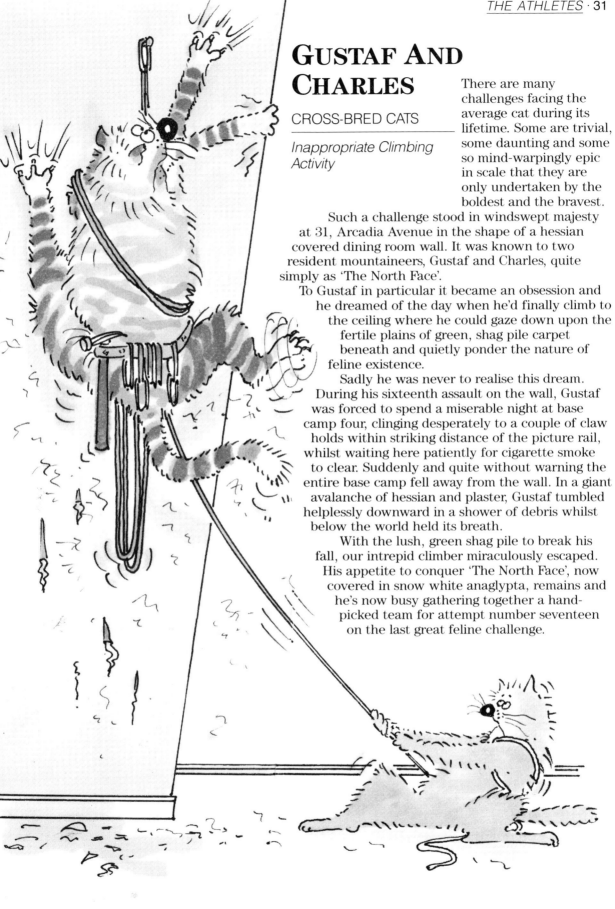

GUSTAF AND CHARLES

CROSS-BRED CATS

Inappropriate Climbing Activity

There are many challenges facing the average cat during its lifetime. Some are trivial, some daunting and some so mind-warpingly epic in scale that they are only undertaken by the boldest and the bravest.

Such a challenge stood in windswept majesty at 31, Arcadia Avenue in the shape of a hessian covered dining room wall. It was known to two resident mountaineers, Gustaf and Charles, quite simply as 'The North Face'.

To Gustaf in particular it became an obsession and he dreamed of the day when he'd finally climb to the ceiling where he could gaze down upon the fertile plains of green, shag pile carpet beneath and quietly ponder the nature of feline existence.

Sadly he was never to realise this dream. During his sixteenth assault on the wall, Gustaf was forced to spend a miserable night at base camp four, clinging desperately to a couple of claw holds within striking distance of the picture rail, whilst waiting here patiently for cigarette smoke to clear. Suddenly and quite without warning the entire base camp fell away from the wall. In a giant avalanche of hessian and plaster, Gustaf tumbled helplessly downward in a shower of debris whilst below the world held its breath.

With the lush, green shag pile to break his fall, our intrepid climber miraculously escaped. His appetite to conquer 'The North Face', now covered in snow white anaglypta, remains and he's now busy gathering together a hand-picked team for attempt number seventeen on the last great feline challenge.

THE SEXUALLY DEVIANT

SAMSON

MONGREL – MALE

Hyper-Sexuality

I suppose all of us from time to time have had the unpleasant experience of having a mutt attempt intercourse with one or both of our carelessly unprotected legs. These attacks usually vary in intensity from high-spirited foreplay to the desperately fierce struggle with the hound whose sexual appetite has endowed him with the strength of a horse!

Such was the case with Samson. One afternoon at a garden party he became consumed with passion for the guest of honour, a highly-placed clergyman. Timing his run with great precision, he mounted a perverted assault of such ferocity on the unfortunate man, that not until he'd been battered by a hundred handbags was he forced to break off the attack.

His owner, destroyed by this sordid episode, now spends most of her time in a darkened room, praying for forgiveness.

SEBASTIAN

COCKER SPANIEL – MALE

Misdirected Hyper-Sexuality

"HOW WAS IT FOR YOU DARLING?"

Preferring partners who could never tax his limited intelligence by answering back, Sebastian, a simple-minded Cocker Spaniel struck up an affair with a golden-haired, brown-eyed beauty known to his family as teddy.

His owner sought help when the children complained that their cuddly toy, a family heirloom and already threadbare, had aged twenty years since embarking on the romance. With the object of his lust banished to the top of the wardrobe after lights out, Sebastian is now making amorous advances to a bright green, life size effigy of Kermit the Frog.

ROLAND

CROSS-BRED CAT – MALE

Trans-Species Sexuality

From the moment he first saw her across a crowded park, Roland fell head over paws in love with Jasmine the Dachshund. Her long, sensuous body, her cold, wet nose, her extremely short but nevertheless shapely legs and her black, beady eyes, all conspired to steal his heart. Ignoring the spiteful whisperings of other cats in the alley, he pursued and won the object of his desires and a passionate relationship developed.

Alas it was to be short-lived. Within a month of their stepping out together, Roland was forced to do the decent thing and end the affair when vicious gossip convinced him that a love between a highborn German aristocrat and a randy old tom from Peckham could never be!

"I LOVE YOU JASMINE!"

ALBERT

CROSS-BRED CAT – MALE

Inappropriate Sexual Behaviour

One enchanted evening, shortly after the central heating installers had finished their work and left for home, Albert glimpsed heaven. Gazing across a crowded living room he spotted what was to become the love of his life. Driven by desire, he casually approached the smooth ebony beauty of the radiator control knob and gently ran his paw across the romantic legend exquisitely engraved around her circumference – 'Higgs & Son Heating and Plumbing Engineers'. She sighed and hissed enticingly and her temperature rose to 78° fahrenheit. Unable to contain himself, Albert grabbed her in a passionate embrace and kissed her roughly. 'I'm sorry', he whispered, 'I shouldn't have done that'. But it was all too late. Her temperature hit 86° and in a frenzy of uncontrollable passion he threw himself upon her. With a violent hissing and bubbling from deep within her pipes, the thermostat peaked at 110° and with 'Higgs & Son Heating and Plumbing Engineers' shimmering with tiny beads of perspiration, a huge wave smashed onto the beach and she melted into Albert's embrace in a glorious oneness of plastic and fur and was his!

LIONEL

CROSS-BRED DOG – MALE

Inappropriate Sexual Behaviour

If there's one thing guaranteed to heap shame and embarrassment on a family, it is having a flasher in its midst. One of the most prolific exponents of this coarse behaviour was a mongrel by the name of Lionel. A seedy looking mutt who spent most of his time lurking in dark corners awaiting the perfect moment to expose his canine credentials, Lionel's timing was always spot on and his sense of occasion superb. Over the years his sad catalogue of indecent acts have included making a sudden appearance on centre stage at a Tupperware party where he stunned a room full of middle-aged ladies and paralysed the hostess, and appearing from behind a bush in a garden causing twenty hungry barbecue guests suddenly to lose interest in food.

Lionel's anti-social behaviour did cease briefly after leaping out of a hedge one evening to flash at a small Yorkshire Terrier he took to be female. The terrier, whose name turned out to be Bruce, instantly returned the compliment, proving himself to be at least three times the dog Lionel could ever hope to be.

The mongrel's ego was dented to such a degree that it was several months before he was able to don his grubby raincoat and climb back into the bushes.

VICTOR

CROSS-BRED CAT – MALE
NEUTERED

Over-Attachment To Owner

WINSTON

ENGLISH BULL
TERRIER – MALE

Misdirected Specific Sexual Response

One of the more bizarre cases on record, concerns Winston, an English Bull Terrier who fell desperately in love with an Electrolux 616 series 2 vacuum cleaner.

Perhaps he was swept off his feet by her smooth, good-looking lines, her gentle hum or her romantic shade of avocado green. It may even have been her ability to vacuum right up to the skirting board that made her so irresistible. Whatever it was, Winston lived in a very dusty house as he refused to share her with the rest of the family.

Cast in the mould of classic voyeur, Victor the ginger tom went to great lengths to spy on the sexual indiscretions of his owner. Even some of his victims admitted to a grudging admiration of his ability to conceal himself silently in the bedroom. Awarding points for the best sexual performances according to the degree of difficulty involved, Victor was rumbled one night by a horrified woman who spotted him grinning down at her from the best seat in the house. Cursing the cat and his owner, she left immediately and not even the knowledge that Victor had awarded her a rare 10 out of 10 for an exquisite performance of the reverse missionary position with double twist, could make her return.

THE 'OUT TO LUNCH' MOB

PONGO

SIAMESE CAT – MALE PICA

Rubber Fixation

A bowl of latex must surely be as far away from the pinnacle of *haute cuisine* as you can get, but to Pongo the Siamese it rated higher than sparrow on the hoof. The thought of a classic Featherlite or a multi-coloured French tickler fresh from its silver pouch would send our gourmet into raptures, and like a hog after truffles, he became an expert at seeking them out. However, things came to a painful head one evening when Pongo, feeling particularly peckish, made a frenzied attempt to claw a late-night snack from where it had just been placed ready to fulfil its intended duty. His owner's howls of pain, heard three streets away, were said by neighbours to be heart-rending and the poor man's sex life was ruined for a month.

Maud, another oriental, preferred snacking on wool rather than rubber. Living by her simple motto, 'you knit it, I'll nibble it', she considered everbody's wardrobe to be a square meal. Eating her family threadbare during the week, she looked forward most of all to Sunday lunch where a typical menu might consist of a 50% wool, 50% polymide sock to start, Cable-knit Sweater *à la* Folk Singer topped with shredded duvet cover to follow, and a simple brace of string vests to finish.

MAUD

SIAMESE CAT – MALE PICA

Wool Fixation

MINNIE

LABRADOR – FEMALE

Separation Anxiety – Destructiveness

Before she was six months old, Minnie already knew the difference between a genuine piece of Chippendale and a genuine piece of chipboard. Belonging to an

antique dealer Minnie had the responsible task of guarding hundreds of priceless bits and pieces ranging from Ming vases to mahogany commodes. However, one day for some inexplicable reason, Minnie began to regard her owner's stock less as *objets d'Art* and more as *objets de Grub*!

Left alone one evening she ate a small walnut foot stool for starters followed by a large Victorian chaise-longue complete with delicious horse-hair stuffing and for dessert an 18th century French still-life surrounded by a delicate Rococo frame simply swimming in gilt.

Minnie's verdict on the antique meal? – Well past it's eat-by date but nevertheless spendidly authentic cuisine!

ELVIS

CROSS-BRED DOG – MALE

Separation Anxiety – Destructiveness

BLACKIE

LABRADOR DOG – MALE

Excessive Appetence

On catching first sight of Blackie it was difficult to determine whether he was a dog or some rare breed of Old English Pig. A deep, rumbling growl as he chewed his way through a brace of cart horse rumps usually gave the game away and a high pitched whining when they were finished confirmed that somewhere beneath the tons of blubber there was in fact a Labrador struggling to get out.

His owners sought help when they were forced to hock the family silver to provide Blackie with what he considered to be a decent snack. Fortunes were won and lost on the London Commodities market when, during one of his blow-outs, the dog scoffed so much that he started a run on soya bean and pork belly futures. That memorable day of frenzied wheeling and dealing is now remembered in city folklore as 'Blackie Monday'.

Elvis also developed a taste for the expensive antique but unlike Minnie, he preferred the exotic, spicy flavours of a good Eastern carpet. Here, he shares with us his recipe for 'Afghan Hotdogs', the ingredients for which he found lying around the floor of his owner's drawing room. This dish can work out to be a touch expensive but the method is simplicity itself.

Take one large Persian carpet (£7,500) and divide neatly into two pieces. Tear one half roughly into small bits and put to one side. Chop two 6′×4′ Afghan rugs (£4,800) finely and mix with Persian pieces. Toss the mixture onto the unused half of the carpet and roll into a long sausage. Season with one or two bits of wall tapestry (£6,500), serve immediately at room temperature and enjoy, enjoy!

FIFI

MONGREL BITCH

Over-Indulgence Induced Dominance

Preferring the good life to a dog's life, Fifi, an overweight hound belonging to a large wealthy household, had her own four-poster bed and a daily menu of which the Roux brothers would have been rightly proud. Spoilt to the extreme, bad-tempered and prone to barking her displeasure at the shortcomings of her staff, Fifi overstepped the mark one day when she leaped out of bed and savaged an elderly butler who'd tried to palm her off with an '82 Chablis instead of the '78.

"HEAVENS ABOVE PHILPOTS NOT ANOTHER BOWL OF LARKS' TONGUES IN ASPIC!!"

SALLY

LABRADOR – BITCH

Insatiable Appetite (Breed Specific)

All guide dogs are trained to ignore every day distractions which might interfere with the job, and put their charges at risk. However, Sally, voted 'Dog Least Likely to Succeed' in the graduating class of '88, forgot her training completely one day when she took off at high speed to bag a Spam sandwich discarded in the gutter across a busy street. From that day on, she became a professional scavenger, dragging her terrified owner recklessly through traffic as she competed with the pigeons for everything from second-hand cheese rolls to second-hand chewing gum. Her passion for snacks on the move prompted British Rail's Catering Division to invite her to star in one of their commercials, but after sampling one of their cheese and cucumber sandwiches, the dog refused point blank on the grounds that she had certain minimum standards to maintain!

THE CHRONICALLY INCONTINENT

FRED, WILLY, TOM, LUKE AND SAMMY

CROSS-BRED CATS

Indoor Territorial Marking

Known collectively as The Wimbledon Formation Spraying Team, they were the greatest exponents ever of the art of cat spraying. All belonging to the same family and living under the same roof they were able to practise twelve hours a day in order to perfect a flawless, synchronised routine. However, the mind-numbing odour resulting from their efforts required so much air freshener that shares in a well-known chemical company rose twenty-nine points on the stock exchange in as many days.

For those of you who've forgotten the heady aroma of cat spray, a scratch 'n' sniff pad is provided overleaf for your enjoyment.

SCRATCH 'N' SNIFF PAD

To remind you of the unmistakable aroma of cat spray, scratch surface of pad, hold close to nose and sniff deeply.

Note: Unfortunately, those of you who are due to have your home and possessions sprayed by a tom cat in the very near future will be unable to detect any smell from this pad.

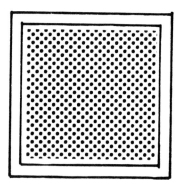

FREDDIE

CROSS-BRED CAT – MALE

Middening

A lover of good television and a stern critic of the bad, Freddie subjected all programmes to his own special quality control system.

Fed up with the endless repeats, unfunny sit-coms and tiresome commercials featuring spotlessly white moggies dipping paws into tins of up-market cat food, Freddie decided to stop the rot. With a radical post-*Watch With Mother* gesture he would register his disapproval by leaving a message on top of the TV set as a smelly reminder to the station chiefs that they really must try harder to improve the service.

To date, *The Guns of Navarone* holds the record for attracting the most attention from Freddie who has performed once on top of the television set for each of the seventeen times it's been repeated.

AND NOW THE FIRST IN OUR SEASON OF FILMS MADE BY THE BULGARIAN MINIMALIST COOPERATIVE. TONIGHT'S SEVEN HOUR EPIC, IN BLACK AND WHITE WITH SUBTITLES, TELLS THE BITTERSWEET STORY OF A YOUNG SPOT-WELDER'S RELATIONSHIP WITH A SHOPPING TROLLEY AND OF HIS STRUGGLE TO COME TO TERMS WITH HIMSELF AND THOSE AROUND HIM WHEN METAL FATIGUE IS DISCOVERED IN THE REAR OFF-SIDE WHEEL.'

NELSON

CROSS-BRED CAT — MALE

Indoor Spraying

It's difficult to pinpoint the exact date when Nelson's political conversion took place but it must have been around the same time as the launching of a string of terrorist attacks on a framed portrait of Tzar Nicholas II and Alexandra.

Hanging proudly on the living room wall to remind its owner of his Russian heritage, the portrait was subjected to a vicious campaign of spraying, responsibility for which was claimed by Nelson on behalf of the 'Glorious Red Mogg Revolutionary Splinter Group for Liberation of the Oppressed Feline Proletariat'. No warning was given before an attack took place but each bore all the hallmarks of the G.R.M.R.S.G.L.O.F.P. A particularly potent brand of spray was used and the targets were always hit squarely between the eyes.

Nelson is currently being sought in connection with the passing on of the secret recipe for Katto-Chunks Supreme Gourmet Delight to a pet food factory in Vladivostock.

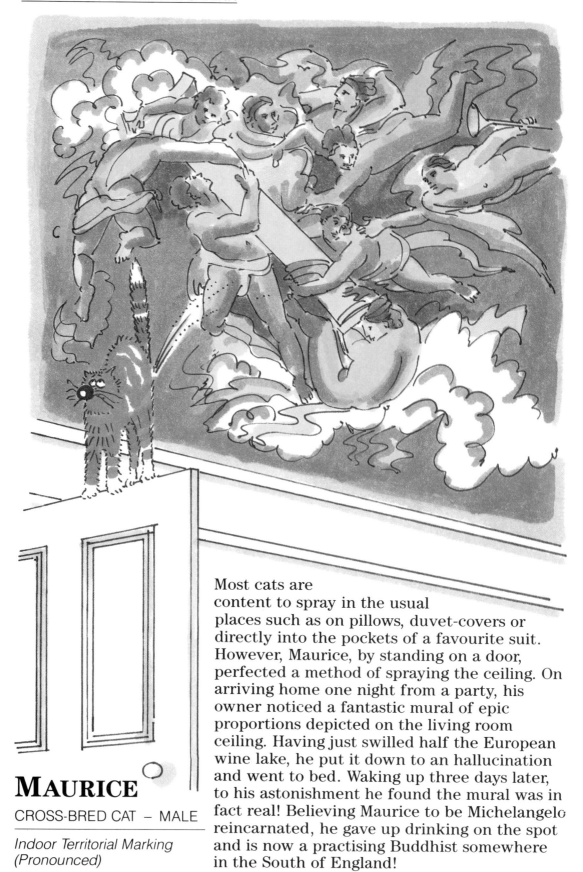

MAURICE

CROSS-BRED CAT – MALE

*Indoor Territorial Marking
(Pronounced)*

Most cats are content to spray in the usual places such as on pillows, duvet-covers or directly into the pockets of a favourite suit. However, Maurice, by standing on a door, perfected a method of spraying the ceiling. On arriving home one night from a party, his owner noticed a fantastic mural of epic proportions depicted on the living room ceiling. Having just swilled half the European wine lake, he put it down to an hallucination and went to bed. Waking up three days later, to his astonishment he found the mural was in fact real! Believing Maurice to be Michelangelo reincarnated, he gave up drinking on the spot and is now a practising Buddhist somewhere in the South of England!

THE TOTALLY DERANGED

RANDOLPH

BULLDOG – MALE

*Idiopathic Aggression
(Possibly Diet Related)*

During the day Randolph was a perfectly normal Bulldog, immersing himself in all the usual activities associated with the breed such as wheezing, panting, slobbering, dribbling and tongue-hanging. However, at 7 pm prompt every evening it all stopped. With a vacant expression crossing his handsome features, Randolph would descend rapidly into a bottomless pit especially reserved for the totally deranged. Growling menacingly at anyone who tried to disturb him, his owners were forced to give the beast a wide berth. Usually lasting an hour, the end of the fit was signalled by a violent twitching of the jowls as Randolph suddenly snapped out of the trance and returned to the world as we know it. Completely unaware of the passage of time and with batteries seemingly recharged, he'd set about his wheezing and slobbering with renewed vigour, stopping only to take another lunch break from reality at 7 pm the following day.

"AT THE THIRD PIP THE TIME WILL BE 7. P.M PRECISELY..."

MOLLY

CROSS-BRED BITCH

*Visual Obsessive Behaviour/
Attention Demanding
Elements Learned*

The sight of a full moon was guaranteed to change Molly from a nice little dog into a nasty little zombie. Totally obsessed with the big silver ball in the sky, on clear nights she'd be out in the back garden keeping the neighbours awake with her constant howling at the Sea of Tranquility. Many people offered explanations for her strange behaviour. There were those who thought she might believe it really was made of cream cheese, a substance for which Molly had a particular weakness, and others who thought she had a secret desire to make the journey one day and take one small step for a dog, one giant step for dogdom. Had the latter been the case, her neighbours, desperate for a night's sleep would gladly have chipped in the funds to provide the rocket!

JOSEPH

MUNSTERLANDER – MALE

Separation Anxiety

Munsterlanders were once used by the German army to sniff out land mines and this probably accounts for the fact that there aren't too many of them around today.

One survivor of the breed was Joseph, a handsome beast who sadly turned out to be a couple of pfennigs short of a Deutschmark.

Agreeing whole-heartedly with Prince Charles that some buildings are monstrous carbuncles, the dog decided to go into the demolition business in a big way and embarked one evening on a huge urban renewal project in his owner's living room. In three hours he reduced furniture, pictures and carpets into a pile of manageable bite-size pieces.

On returning home, his owner, slightly annoyed as he'd not granted planning permission, threw the book at the dog, closely followed by bits of what had once been his bookcase.

Joseph, whose name has since been put forward for service in a German infantry regiment now lives in exile, a misunderstood developer dreaming of plans to demolish the Royal Crescent at Bath and build a 'white knuckle' theme park in its place.

HERBIE

WHIPPET – MALE

Single Trauma-Induced General Nervousness

Only slightly less timid than a harvest mouse, the fragile nerves of Herbie the Whippet were finally shattered one day by a thunderous crack and a fearful hissing that could only mean Armageddon was close at hand. So it was that a careless neighbour, opening a can of slightly sparkling mineral water in the garden next door, was responsible for Herbie's disappearance under his owner's bed and for his decision to stay there for the rest of his life.

One enjoyable spin-off from this sad tale was that Herbie's trembling, transmitted through the brass frame, provided the amorous occupants above with the only vibrating bed in Macclesfield.

RONNIE

CROSS-BRED DOG – MALE

Phobic (Light bulbs)

Lying on a rug one evening in front of a gently burning log fire, Ronnie wandered the back streets of that strange, dream-like state somewhere between waking and sleeping. With eyes half-closed, jowls in spasm and nose a-twitch, he sighed heavily, as he speculated on the possibilities of an amorous encounter with the racy-looking Basset Hound who'd just moved in next door.

Suddenly, quite without warning and with a blast equivalent to seven tons of TNT., a sixty watt lightbulb exploded in the standard lamp above Ronnie's head, and in one movement, he was up and running.

After a violent collision with a closed door which registered 7.8 on a nearby university seismograph, the dog turned and took off blindly through a window, which was mercifully open.

Three days later, seventy miles from home and still running, Ronnie was finally overhauled in the fast lane of the M1, after a police chase across three counties.

Now back home, ruined by his experience, he sleeps fitfully in a darkened room, plagued by a recurring nightmare where he becomes trapped in a British Home Store's lighting department, cornered by a huge unruly mob of 100 watt, screw-fit spot lights tormenting him through the night with threats of spontaneous combustion.

BENJI

MASTIFF – MALE

Specific Phobia Induced By Owner Related Aggression

Walking to his food bowl one evening, Benji happened to step on an upturned push button telephone, and by so doing, unwittingly dialled the speaking clock in Kuala Lumpur. When a £4,606 phone bill arrived a month later, his owner, a deep shade of purple, foaming at the mouth and screaming abuse, stood in front of the bewildered dog, pointed to the telephone and delivered a size 12 boot into Benji's rear end. Struggling to make sense of this mindless violence from his usually docile owner, the dog came to the conclusion that it could only be demonic possession and that somehow the telephone was responsible.

From that day forth, Benji regarded all telephones as Beelzebub's foot soldiers and the telephone box, glowing in the dark at the end of the street, as The Prince of Darkness himself.

BILLY

MONGREL – MALE

Separation Anxiety: Symptom: Howling

With a fan club boasting membership from as far afield as the next street, Billy the mongrel was regarded by friends and admirers as one of the all time great exponents of the canine twelve bar blues. A singer-songwriter with an extraordinary lack of pedigree, Billy, known on the street as 'Boxcar', would often howl the blues into the wee small hours causing his family to suffer much in the name of Art. Below is his classic 'Ol' Mongrel Blues'.

WELL I WOKE UP THIS MORNIN'
HEARD SOME REAL BAD NEWS
MY MAMA'S GOT DISTEMPER
AN' MY DADDY'S ON THE BOOZE
MY WOMAN'S RUN OFF WITH A BULLDOG
MAN I GOT THEM OLD MONGREL BLUES.

WELL MY GRANDPA'S DOWN WITH HARDPAD
AN' GRANNY'S GOT THE SAME
MY BROTHER'S IN THE DOG POUND
MY BEST FRIEND'S GONE INSANE
ONE SISTER'S STRUNG OUT ON DOGGIE CHOCS
AN' THE OTHER'S ON THE GAME.

WELL I WOKE UP THIS MORNIN'
HEARD SOME REAL BAD NEWS
CAME LAST AGAIN IN THE DOG SHOW
GUESS I WAS BORN TO LOSE
THEY SAY I'VE GOT NO BREEDIN'
BUT I'VE SURE GOT THEM OLD MONGREL BLUES.
AWOOOOO HOOOOOO

TINKERBELL

CROSS-BRED CAT – MALE

Inter-Species Aggression

Tinkerbell got along well with everyone in the neighbourhood except George, a high lumbering Bull Mastiff with whom she was forced to share the same house. She considered the dog to be ugly, smelly and in terms of refinement only one step up the evolutionary ladder from a jar of plankton.

One day, driven to distraction by the dog's loutish behaviour, Tinkerbell decided to teach him a lesson and donning sequined trunks and a silk dressing gown, the 5lb 4oz moggie stepped into the ring to go fifteen rounds with the 123lb mutt.

Pundits of the fight game were predicting the contest would never go the distance as the bell sounded for the first round. The dog, a slow lumbering south paw charged out of his corner swinging wildly but Tinkerbell's counter punching was crisp, stylish and accurate. It was clear from the outset that the hound had underestimated his opponent.

Within two minutes, George was covering up on the ropes in a desperate attempt to stay on his paws as the moggie unloaded a vicious combination of jabs and hooks. With thirty seconds still to go and the dog hanging on, praying for the end of the round, Tinkerbell stepped back, performed a perfect Ali-shuffle and unleashed a brain-squashing upper cut that sent the hound's jowls into spasm and his gum-shield spinning into the crowd. At this point, the owner stepped in to save the dog further punishment and the fight was stopped.

There have been fifteen rematches since and with Tinkerbell's record standing at fifteen wins from fifteen fights, all inside the distance, she's now first in line for a crack at the world title currently held by 'The Prince of Darkness' (Page 54).

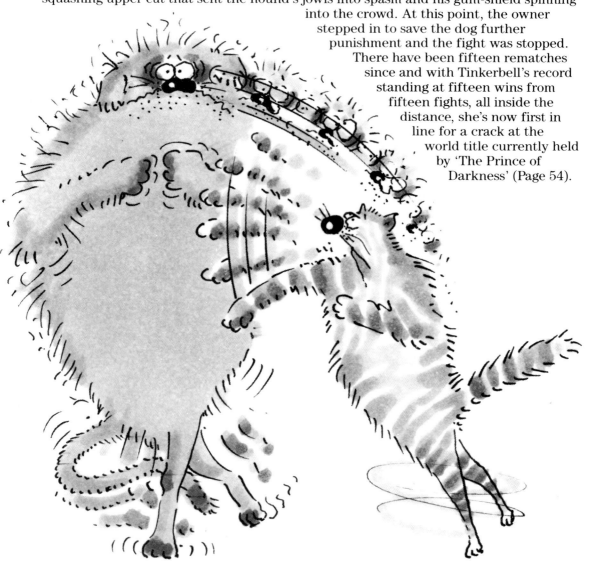

JAMES

CROSS-BRED CAT – MALE

Social Detachment

Just as some human beings decide to drop out of the rat-race so James decided one day to drop out of the cat-race. Saying a fond farewell to his family, he eased himself through the catflap for the last time and without looking back strode off into the garden to become a hippy.

Having found a sheltered spot with good vibes under an apple tree, he pitched camp and sat down for a few months to contemplate his navel.

In the quietness of this far-out scene he pondered many things from the shortcomings of the material world and its cat-eat-cat mentality to the shallowness of a life revolving around a bowl of Katto-Chunks a day and a plastic mouse on the end of a piece of elastic.

Accepting only the odd bowl of milk supplied by the Salvation Army whose meeting hall was next door, James somehow found the strength to write a text book entitled, 'A Moggy's Guide to Roots and Berries', but so far the tome has proved very unpopular in feline circles.

THE HEAVY GANG

TYSON

CROSS-BRED CAT – MALE

*Despotic Aggression,
Highly Territorial*

A huge, fearsome tabby whose exterior consisted of 50% fur and 50% scar tissue, Tyson, suspected by his owner of being some sort of feline contract killer, devoted his life entirely to violence and mayhem. The leader of organised crime in the tough city of Windsor, Berkshire, where only the fit survive, the sight of him swaggering down the alleyways with his stunning-looking but brain-dead Siamese moll on one arm and a couple of heavy-looking ginger toms bringing up the rear, struck fear and loathing into every decent law-abiding moggie in the neighbourhood.

Suspected of homicide and racketeering, Tyson is currently wanted by the authorities for beating up a mincing Peke-Faced Persian and stealing his electronic cat-flap opener.

Walter Higgins, a green parrot with blood-red patches around his jowls was regarded by many to be the most evil creature ever to swing on a perch. Inspired by the endless television repeats of Hitchcock's *The Birds*, Walter's speciality was launching full frontal attacks on the throats of visitors to his house. His owner, fearing that one day Walter might strike his intended target, the jugular vein, and send a dear friend into the after-life, sentenced him to solitary confinement in a maximum security cage.

Walter, now doing bird, divides his time between whittling Cuttle

"THERE AIN'T NO CAGE BIN BUILT NOWHERE WHAT CAN HOLD WALTER 'PRETTY BOY' 'IGGINS!! YA HEAR ME!? <u>NO</u> CAGE NOWHERE!!!!"

WALTER

GREEN PARROT – MALE

*Territorial Aggression
(Pronounced)*

Fish bone, screaming threats of unspeakable violence at his family and looking forward to the day he can escape and carry them out.

BILL AND BEN

DACHSHUNDS – MALE

*Intermale Dominance
Aggression*

Thinking a couple of dogs would be a welcome distraction for her guests, the owner of a retirement home for elderly gentlefolk took delivery of a brace of Dachshunds, each from different kennels. Within seconds of meeting, Bill and Ben decided they hated each other and before a gentlefolk could so much as scratch their backs, they were locked in a titanic struggle that was to last six months. Pausing only for food and the occasional trot through the dayroom to seek tactical advice from interested residents, the two beasts finally got their marching orders one day when, during the seventh round of a scheduled fifteen-rounder, they became entangled in a walking frame belonging to a guest. It took four gentlefolk working through the night to separate them and when finally the last coil was untangled the dogs were shipped off immediately to their new homes.

Bill now lives happily in Land's End and Ben in John o'Groats.

ROGUES' GALLERY

I present here five police mug-shots of the evil hounds who stand at the top of the country's most wanted list. If spotted they should not be approached under any circumstances as all are considered armed and dangerous.

WANTED

WILFRED
ALIAS
THE PRINCE OF DARKNESS
WHITE ENGLISH BULL TERRIER

4791420

Distinguishing features: scar tissue on cheeks and snout. Tattoo on right forearm reads 'Mother'. Last seen in Walthamstow, London. Wanted for homicide, kidnapping and extortion.

BILLY
ALIAS
THE SHIFTY LITTLE TOAD
BROWN MONGREL

6460017

Distinguishing features: three scars on right cheek. One front leg slightly shorter than the other. Last seen robbing a butcher's shop in Portsmouth. Wanted for fraud, embezzlement, theft and assault with a deadly weapon.

ROCKY
ALIAS
THE HIT MAN
RHODESIAN RIDGEBACK

0976210

Distinguishing marks: snout is two thirds scar tissue. One claw missing from left foot. Tattoo on right arm reads 'I hate everybody and everybody hates me'. Last seen in Liverpool. Wanted for racketeering and a string of public order offences.

ROGER
ALIAS
THE DUMBELL
GREY MONGREL

774320

Distinguishing marks: patch of mange on rump. Very high on muscle, very low on brains. Last seen robbing a milk float in Sheffield. Wanted for a series of armed robberies and Grievous Bodily Harm.

HERMAN
ALIAS
THE WIDOW MAKER
BLACK ROTTWEILER

0173061

Distinguishing features: numerous scars on snout. Death's Head and SS serial number tattooed inside left ear. Barks with a German accent. Last seen in Cardiff trying to board a ship for South America. Wanted for crimes against humanity.

BRUCE

BLACK LABRADOR – MALE

MR X

PROMINENT EXECUTIVE – MALE

Dominance Aggression Towards Other Male Dogs

According to those whose job it is to know, there are few members of the Kennel Club more aggressive when in the mood than a Black Labrador. Such an animal was Bruce, a malevolent beast always on the lookout for a rumble in the local park. His owner, Mr X, became fed up with the dog's aggression and sought help from a book written by animal trainer Barbara Woodhouse. She guaranteed that a finger placed into a dog's rear-end would bring the most frenzied attack to a shuddering halt. Overcoming an understandable reluctance to follow this advice, Mr X tried it and found to his delight that it did indeed work! He used this technique to great effect until one night in the park, Bruce set about an opponent who turned out to be another Black Labrador. They joined battle with equal enthusiasm. Mr X set to work and after an heroic struggle he managed to apply his method not only to Bruce but also to the other dog and, keeping the peace in this compromising position, he was discovered by the Parks Pervert Patrol who'd crept up on him over the grass in size fourteen boots!

Mr X defended himself in the subsequent trial and his pleas of mercy in a closing speech lasting two hours longer than the Gettysburg Address, reduced the jury to tears and thankfully he was acquitted of all charges.

EVENIN' ALL

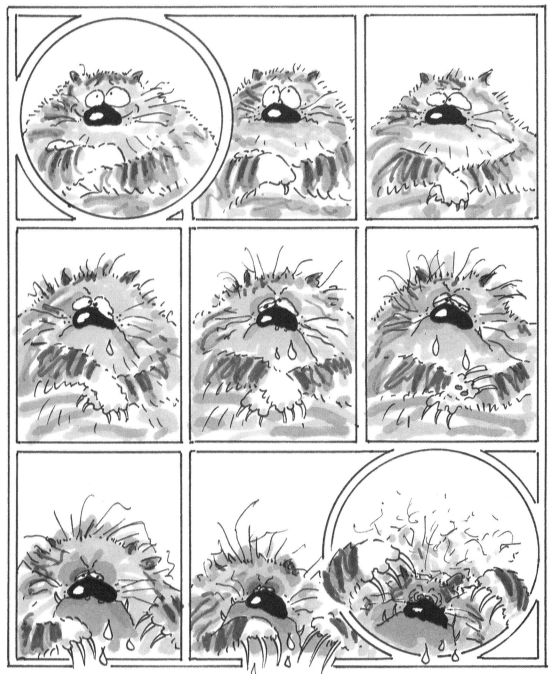

ROMMEL

CROSS-BRED CAT – MALE

Idiopathic Aggression

Having witnessed the Jekyll and Hyde change that regularly afflicted Rommel, his owner was tragically reduced to little more than a vegetable. Her mind completely scrambled she finds the terrifying experiences too horrible to describe in words. However, from her foetal position on the floor, where she rocks slowly back and forth, sucking her thumb and humming a strangely haunting tune, she's managed to draw the pictures which give a disturbing insight into her dreadful ordeal.

NORMAN

CROSS-BRED DOG – MALE

Specific Aggression

From an early age Norman made it perfectly clear that he hated black people. His racism was so extreme that in an effort to uncover the reasons for it his owner investigated the dog's background to see if there might be some South African connections but none could be found. The dog seemed to harbour most hatred for Rastafarians and the sight of a large woolly hat and dreadlocks would send him into a frenzy of loathing and many an expensive ghettoblaster had been dropped in panic by a fleeing Rasta trying desperately to stay one step ahead of a very fast dog.

Norman's hatred was not confined to black people. He also hated black dogs and it was one such beast that brought his career as a racist to an abrupt end when one afternoon Norman tried to impose white supremacy on a particularly mean black labrador. There ensued an almost exact re-enactment of The Battle of Rorke's Drift from which Norman took several weeks to recover.

His owner reported that following the fight his dog seemed to lose interest in racism and soon after gave up his membership of the Kanine Klu Klux Klan.

DANNY

CROSS-BRED DOG – MALE

Kennelosis

Before his owners left for their annual two weeks of relaxation in the peaceful Mediterranean backwater of Torremolinos, Danny was the perfect pet. Friends and neighbours couldn't speak highly enough of the good natured tail wagger and his list of virtues was endless. He'd fetch his owner's slippers from the bedroom, walk him to the pub and guide him back again. He'd carry newspapers and packages from the shops, chase sticks and dive fearlessly into rivers in pursuit of stones. He was sweetness and light to visitors and he loved children.

He never had fleas or mange, never slobbered or broke wind and never indulged in barnyard sex. He never complained about the food and indeed, has his owner wished it, Danny would even have attempted to tackle a British Rail Snak-pak with a smile on his face.

However, after two weeks in boarding kennels whilst his owners were falling off bar stools in Spain it was clear that Danny had picked up one or two bad habits.

Within an hour of returning home he'd slobbered on the furniture, indulged in a bizarre sexual act and attempted to murder 2 cats, 3 dogs, a pet rabbit and a postman. Following this experience, the family toyed with the idea of taking Danny with them on holiday the following year, but decided against this when they realised the dog could pick up some really nasty habits during two weeks in Torremolinos.

SIMON

GOLDEN COCKER SPANIEL –
MALE

Rage Syndrome

A rare condition considered by most progressive veterinary surgeons up until 1987 to be demonic possession, Rage Syndrome is a terrifying spectacle to witness. The symptoms of waking up, flying into a blind rage and returning to sleep in the space of half a minute are demonstrated by Simon the Spaniel, a chronic sufferer. Thankfully, his fits were always proceeded by a bout of fierce nose twitching, allowing his family time to run panic-stricken into the garden where they'd wait quietly until the sounds of snoring indicated the attack was over.

IVAN

CROSS-BRED CAT – MALE
NEUTERED

*Fear-Induced Now Learned
Aggression Towards Children*

Despising anybody under four feet in height, particularly if wearing a school uniform, Ivan the Terrible quite simply hated children. This deranged moggie would spend his days roaming the grounds of a primary school, conveniently located next door to his house, seeking out the weakest, most vulnerable of the pupils. The sight of small, desperate figures running in terror across the playground with a ginger tom attached like a limpet to gymslip or blazer became commonplace. The Parent Teachers Association sought help when the school bus was headed off at the pass by Ivan, who almost managed to claw his way through the sheet steel roof before some skilful but violent manoeuvring by the terrified driver managed to dislodge him!

SCHOOL BUS

JOEY

CROSS-BRED CAT – MALE

Despotic Aggression

An orphan wandering the city streets, Joey was taken in by the owner of an illegal gambling den in London's Chinatown and put to work as a mouser. It was here amongst the mahjong chips, egg foo yong and clouds of strange smelling blue smoke that the cat learned the secrets of the feline Tongs and became a 49th Dan in Moggie Jitsu.

He was taught how to dessicate a building block with one head butt, how to appreciate a great chop suey and how to indulge in tyranny on a grand scale.

When the gambling den was closed down, Joey went to live with an elderly couple who had retired to the country and it was here in the fields surrounding his new home that he gained a reputation that made Pol Pot seem like Mother Theresa's spiritual advisor.

Together with a motley crew of strays from a nearby farm, he embarked on a campaign of terror the likes of which the local peasantry had never seen before. Within two weeks the countryside was barren, its population having fled in panic from the ginger despot who now ruled with an iron fist.

Professional help was sought and action taken when the owner of a neighbouring farm complained that he was unable to accept any more of the refugee wildlife that had been streaming in long dishevelled lines towards the border and the haven of his cornfield which lay next door.

Joey is currently taking an enforced break from sack and pillage but is believed by his elderly owners to be secretly plotting a second cultural revolution with his motley crew.

THE ACID TEST

When filled in, the questionnaire below will give you an indication of the state of your pet's mental health. It's important that you respond to all the questions truthfully.

When you've completed your answers refer to the bottom of the page to see how your pet has scored.

1. Does your dog or cat prefer eating:
  A. Tinned food ☐
  B. A mixture of tinned food and scraps ☐
  C. Brillo pads ☐

2. When you scold your pet for wrong-doing does he:
  A. Get the message immediately and behave ☐
  B. Get the message after a short while and then behave ☐
  C. Secretly relieve himself in your stereo headphones and wait for you to put them on ☐

3. When you take your dog for a walk does he:
  A. Usually behave ☐
  B. Sometimes behave ☐
  C. Embarrass you by attempting sexual intercourse with each of the sixty people in the Post Office queue ☐

4. When visitors call round does your dog:
  A. Give them a genuinely warm welcome ☐
  B. Give them a polite but slightly aloof welcome ☐
  C. Give them forty stitches in one buttock and a painful tetanus jab in the other ☐

5. At bedtime does your dog or cat
  A. Drop off to sleep on a favourite cushion or blanket ☐
  B. Drop off to sleep anywhere ☐
  C. Drop off the top of the wardrobe onto your bed and insist on a fight to the death ☐

If you've ticked mainly C's, your pet is a perfectly normal animal.

If you've ticked mainly B's, your pet is a borderline case and a close watch should be kept on him.

If you've ticked mainly A's, then I'm sorry to have to tell you that your pet is just the sort of candidate who is likely to end up on Peter Neville's couch.

EPILOGUE

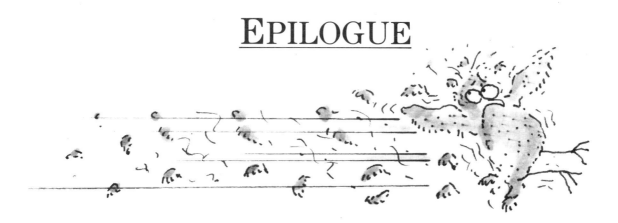

BY PETER NEVILLE

So there you have it. A short run through the asylum of animal lunacy from my casebooks with the incredibly talented Russell Jones.

I must reassure you that all the cases represented in this book are indeed true in origin. I have actually treated nervous eagles (well, one anyway!), dangerous dogs, feather-plucking parrots, all kinds of canine and feline aggressors and those suffering from separation anxiety. They represent a cross-section of my patients, most of whom I'm pleased to say are now cured or have had their excesses reduced to tolerable levels. Some of course take longer than others to improve. Ivan the Terrible (page 61) will now tolerate older children but still gets aggressively excited when toddlers appear, while Dylan (page 21) has learned the futility of guarding dustbins and that waiting politely for his lunch is a more rewarding pastime. Gone are the beautiful brown stain frescoes of Maurice (page 44), and the rehoming of Willy caused a swift decline in bookings for the Wimbledon Formation Spraying Team (page 41). Mr X can now walk Bruce (page 56) at sensible times of the day safe in the knowledge that other dogs are no longer at risk and that he can now safely return to his old habit of nail-biting! Marty (page 17) has also learned the error of his ways and now finds life bearable without the self-administered jolts of electro-convulsive therapy so important to him before. Roland (page 33) has ceased his wayward sexual behaviour now that the Dachshund in his life no longer comes into season. But sadly many of the strange feline diners simply have to remain in wool- or rubber-free rooms. Research is continuing as we say.

Such behaviour problems can be modified by a variety of means. Phobic desensitisation, controlled exposure, positive and negative conditioning, surgical intervention, hormonal management and sedatives all have their role in treating those animals with problems. An aggressive response to anti-social behaviour is usually counter-productive and is never employed in my practice. Successful treatment comes with understanding, kindness and patience, but in order to apply any of these and iron out the wrinkles in an otherwise adorable pet, you are going to need a sense of humour!

Confession time. Bullet (page 20) and Colonel (page 12) have not had their names changed as they both belong to me. Well, since builders' houses fall down and doctors' children fall ill you would hardly expect an animal behavourist to have normal pets would you?!